THE DOG IN THE SKY

Helen Ivory was born in Luton in 1969, and lives in Norwich. She has worked in shops, behind bars, on building sites and with several thousand free-range hens. She has studied painting and photography and has a Degree in Cultural Studies from Norwich School of Art. In 1999 she won an Eric Gregory Award.

Her first collection *The Double Life of Clocks* was published by Bloodaxe Books in 2002. She was given an Arts Council Writer's Award in 2005 and is now Academic Director and teacher of Creative Writing for Continuing Education at the University of East Anglia. *The Dog in the Sky* (Bloodaxe Books, 2006) is her second collection.

HELEN IVORY

The Dog
in the Sky

BLOODAXE BOOKS

Copyright © Helen Ivory 2006

ISBN: 1 85224 717 7

First published 2006 by
Bloodaxe Books Ltd,
Highgreen,
Tarset,
Northumberland NE48 1RP.

www.bloodaxebooks.com
For further information about Bloodaxe titles
please visit our website or write to
the above address for a catalogue.

Bloodaxe Books Ltd acknowledges
the financial assistance of
Arts Council England, North East.

Cover printing by J. Thomson Colour Printers Ltd, Glasgow.

Printed in Great Britain by
Bell & Bain Limited, Glasgow.

For Martin, my love

ACKNOWLEDGEMENTS

Acknowledgements are due to the editors of the following publications in which some of these poems first appeared: *Mslexia*, *Reactions 5* (Pen & Inc, 2005) and *The Wolf*.

I would like to thank Martin Figura, George Szirtes, Sarah Law, Esther Morgan, Tom Corbett, Café Writers and Mike Thurman for their help and support. I would also like to thank Arts Council England for a Writer's Award given in 2005, John Hambley for nominating me and Kate Pullinger for her help.

CONTENTS

Kite

She is on the edge of land, can go no further
She throws an anchor to the sky,
looks up in prayer, the wind at the nape of her neck.

This worrying, this breeze creeps upon her
like a soggy blanket blown in from the arctic coast.
Her hands hold the anchor fast.

This is the wish she has for herself;
let clouds bury this satellite, deep.
Let the fishes of the sky welcome this message

and recognise the writing as their own.
Let she become weightless as the sound of a feather
spelling out the shape of her name.

Let this chill be removed from her.
Let it be now, let it be now.

Shoreline

There are times like this
when the ache of you
fills the pit of my stomach.

When the person
following the shoreline
could be you.

Your hands are thrust
deep inside your pockets
as you warm pebbles

like worry stones.
There is a whole beach
of them to count.

I watch the woman
with the too big dog
pulling her towards the sea.

I watch her try to keep upright
as she sinks ankle-deep
into the small sharp stones.

Offering

This is her heart –
a chipped
piece of glass.

She is holding it
in her hand. She is
offering it to you.

Curled like a sigh,
cutting corners licked tame
by the sea; a boiled sweet.

She is standing quite still,
the wind whips her hair
across her face.

Through the glass
you can see her fingers,
shadows, blood.

China Blue

In her mouth she put
all her words,
and handfuls of earth to bury them,
her best shoes that were red
and not to his taste,
and most of the music
she had ever liked.

Then for many years
she kept her mouth quite shut.
Until one day she put in a map
of everywhere she'd ever been
with him, and set it alight
so she'd never in a million years
find her way back again, ever.

When it was time
to spit all of this out
she found that everything
had turned to glitter and diamonds,
had put on roller-skates,
skedaddling off
into the china blue.

Knowing

I am at the edge of my knowing;
there is no geography to describe
what happens next to my feet.
How do I decide to step,
to not step? I sense the weight
of gravity below me; coquettish
and inviting, utterly without guile.

Clouds would at least give an illusion
of landscape, but the sky below me
at the edge of the world is faultlessly blue.
And anyway, for some reason
I am already standing on some sea or other.
Fishes are tickling my toes, nudging me forward.
They are leaping, and seem to be giggling.

Learning to Talk

I pretend not to notice
this new language I'm learning;
let it creep up on me
timid, like a feral cat.

If I wrap my tongue around it
like a lasso, surely
it will try to get away, ·
balk, lash out.

And so I wait
for the low gentle purr
to rise in my throat. I wait.
I wait for these words

to talk to you, my love.
Already the claws have retracted,
already the soft pads of my feet
itch to be tickled.

Element

I think I have discovered
the hundred and seventeenth element.
I've been saving a space especially
on the sketched-out edge of things.

I know its weight,
feel its gravity;
its restlessness,
its itching to be something else.

It's in the air we breathe in and out
to each other, in love;
passing particles of low heaven
like a clever game of catch.

Alchemy

Seasoned with a little fire
I am quicksilver in your mouth.
Drink me down, I am pure enough,
the colour of sky in water.

This could be a good thing for you –
think of it as an experiment.
You don't even need to do anything,
just accept me into your body.

You will feel a freedom, a fluidity even.
There will be no pain, only light,
the kind that floods into every
undiscovered part of your soul.

This may seem dramatic, absurd even –
and a certain amount of trust is required.
But don't worry – I am only a woman;
commonplace, like the moon, like breathing.

Listen only to your breathing

Listen only to your breathing,
to my breathing and you will find
this room will lose its corners,

walls, ceiling; the windows
will open wide, and you will feel yourself
drifting towards the sky

which will not be sky.
You must listen only to your breathing
to my breathing, as the warm liquid

sky surrounds us and draws us
deep into the clouds
which will not be clouds

which will only feel like clouds
as you take them on your tongue
and swallow them whole.

And the taste will be beyond sweetness;
will be inside us as you breathe,
as I breathe, as we breathe.

Sweetness

The air is thick with peach light
and I am drunk on its juices
like a little girl who's eaten
too much chocolate.

Headiness bounces
from the red-painted walls
voluptuously, brazenly,
and squashes itself into the corners

which say nothing – it is hard
to talk with your mouth full.
And so much sweetness!
Sweetness abounds! Sweetness unbounds!

The corners and me,
we just loll onto our backs.
With smiling eyes, we drink a toast
to the ceiling and all other heights.

Friday Night Tango

Monday and everyone's
just arrived.
Most have never danced before,
nothing like this
with proper steps.
Alison has bought new shoes.

By Tuesday
she has mastered
a couple of the basic steps.
Her partner is a perfect stranger
and this is the closest
she's ever been to anyone.

The scent of his skin
is hard to wash from her hands.
Wednesday night
is spent sleeplessly.
The curlers she's bought to tame her hair
keep uncurling

and Thursday she wakes
on a pillow of pins
in a mass of snakes.
She spends ages
looking for the skull cap
she wears on these occasions.

Friday comes round so soon
but they are ready
for tonight, her partner and she.
Fluid, the teacher says that morning,
as they cover the floor
with new learned steps.

Friday night and there's a band,
but all you can really hear
is the swish of feet
on the wooden floor
and the low gentle hiss
of Alison's heavily lacquered hair.

Pinocchio's Sister

Pinocchio's sister trips the light fantastic,
itching to cut loose of her strings.
These are heady times; the air glows
with strobes and fireflies; this is something else.

Her little wooden head is burning
with so many new tastes and sights and sounds
that she just doesn't know what to do
with these awkward limbs,

not to mention the strings,
which she is thinking of taking a match to.
And when she does, she will refuse
to bend over backwards into cliché any more.

Leave that to the puppet master, she says
crinkling her button nose just a tad.

How it is

We must begin to tell the children lies.
The fire starts to chuckle in the grate,
and so we turn away from trusting eyes.

The story that we tell them simply tries
to let a little light in, though it's late;
we must begin to tell the children lies.

Though listening close they'll not see the disguise;
the masks and veils we wear – what we create
when we turn away from trusting eyes.

By this fireside they'll not realise
the snow outside is blocking off the gate.
We must begin to tell the children lies.

Why need you feel you must apologise –
of course it's right to shield them from their fate.
And so we turn away from trusting eyes.

We should work hard to muffle up their cries
before they're even uttered – let's not wait.
We must begin to tell the children lies.
And so we turn away from trusting eyes.

Talking

Someone said something about the moon, I think.
There was talk of waxing and waning,
of constellations, of the whole magnitude of things,
how we are not in control of our destiny,
that *destiny*, by its very definition
is something that controls us, and not vice versa.

The fire crackled and someone poured some more whisky.
Then someone began talking about cheese,
how it's made, the curdling and the wheying,
how it must be pasteurised
and left for a good long while to mature
before you can even think of eating it.

Nobody said anything for quite some time after that.

The Dog and the Magpie

Dog said it was OK, but Magpie begged to differ.
These are strange times when you can't trust your own dog.
Out of the blue things crash through your mind
like startled sheep by the roadside,
who for all their softness, jut their horned heads
into the mousy sky, almost piercing the clouds.

But Dog keeps up his good cheer, trotting blindly beside you
despite the piebald cries, despite the sheep
who have now created quite a stampede.
It's OK, he says, it's OK. But even then you can't help
noticing how he's not looking you straight in the eye;
how he keeps glancing over his shoulder.

The Little Dog of Darkness

Darkness moves through the streets,
a little dog trotting at its heels.
The dog sees the shadows
that Darkness doesn't.

He sees inside flats and bedsits
where food rots in cupboards
and masked ladies apply
powder with *faux* rabbits' feet.

He sees the man that Darkness
only hears coughing;
can see the yellowing spots
in the whites of his eyes.

With alert little ears,
this dog hears every transaction
as his paws skitter-skat
past alleys and untaxed cars,

past the fake breasted woman
whose open-mouthed laugh
seems to swallow the whole world
then, gasping for air, spits it out,

smelling faintly of lipstick
and the used taste of money.
The little dog of Darkness says nothing.
He is, after all, his master's dog

and slow cataracts
take more away each day,
and dogs have short memories,
or so he likes to believe.

Persona

I have not always been able to speak so freely.
There have been, shall we say,
certain limitations on my actions.
You see, for years I was a wolf,
shuffling dejectedly
around the fringes of the human world.

People saw no reason for my night time
perambulations or moonlit laments.
My snufflings around graveyards
confounded them.
But deep down, I knew my body
was hidden somewhere.

It all got rather messy,
and to cut a long story short,
restrictions were put upon me
banning me from my regular haunts.
Documents were passed above my head
I was deemed unfit to sign.

The hunt for my body;
my true body, my furless, fangless,
human form could not end there,
in that place of high windows
and regulated mealtimes.
And so I planned my escape.

I trained myself to walk on two legs,
and with a little more effort,
began to form words in my lupine throat.
The people around me responded favourably,
striking up conversations
about my life before wolfdom, and such.

Papers were signed and I was released.
And now my search has begun in earnest.
I find a simple *Good Evening*,
or the calling to heel of imaginary dogs
throws people off the scent
in graveyards late at night.

Snow

It was noon on Tuesday when it began to snow
and by Wednesday morning the whole street
was sparkling white like a fresh washed sheet.
And Thursday took away the car entirely so
if we did leave the house, all we had were our feet.
Friday and the door was blocked so we couldn't go

anywhere, even if we could think of anywhere to go.
It's strange how memory is covered up with snow
when the last time you remember using your feet
was this morning when you got out of bed. The street
and what's beyond doesn't figure at all, except in the so
so distant past when you think you remember a sheet

covered ghost of a place you used to visit. The sheet
hardly sparkles, unlike the white outside, which doesn't go
and is still growing, replacing even the sky, it is so
huge. I do wonder though, if this malaise is more than snow.
If something more malevolent is lurking in the street
and making us forget how to put shoes on our feet.

It's weekend I think. Today I've been looking at my feet;
I noticed something strange when I peeled back the sheet.
Yours too were a little odd. I wonder if others in the street
have similar problems. Maybe we should find our shoes, go
next door, pay a neighbourly visit, but it's the snow
that melts our resolve. And there is the ever so

little problem with our feet, which have become so
much like jelly it is really difficult to stand up. Feet
are only part of the problem. It seems that the snow
has somehow affected our ability to talk. Blank sheets
of unwritten dialogue hang around in the air, nowhere to go
except to maybe end up as litter in the street.

Unlike us. It looks unlikely we will ever see the street
again. Although it doesn't matter; we cannot even so
much as utter the word, or remember what it is, let alone go.
There's nothing to do now but watch our feet
jellyfish. And the rest of our bodies, if we lift the sheet
have gone the same way. This is all since the snow.

There is no noise from the street. No feet walk anywhere,
not even in our heads. So, this is it. This sheet of nothingness
which is not snow, holds in its breath, will not let go.

The Dog in the Sky

When the poor dog
was walking in snow
he circled widdershins
sniffing for a patch

that was not bleached,
that smelled of earth,
that didn't dust his coat
with white raw cold.

No luck,
he turned towards the grain
in wider circles
orbiting his original prints.

Listing,
he turned to the stars
for direction
as it was now quite dark.

And it seems
they talked him out
of the earth;
of ever seeing or wanting it again.

For now his paw-prints
glitter the sky
willy-nilly,
almost passing for stars.

Nancy's Dream

Her dead husband is learning to fly.
Daylight flights are fine
but it's wartime, so night flights
are impossible with the black-outs.

She's fretting about how he will ever land
and when the sirens go off
she worries about how they know
these are enemy planes overhead.

He could be up there, in the middle
of all the stars and the moon-washed clouds
with the carrier pigeons whose homes
have been destroyed by the bombing.

He could be up there with a lock of her hair
in that envelope scented with lavender
flying aimlessly in the dark,
and not being able to land, not ever.

Dark Energy

Space is getting bigger.
It breathes
down your neck,
holds a knife to your throat,
will take no prisoners.

The stars on the ceiling
are spiralling, lost,
bashing against the woodchip,
scattering
to the exploded corners of the room.

Gravity is losing its hold
on everything.
You pull the duvet
over your head
as if this cluster of matter

will be enough.

Matter

Merely explaining how
our ever expanding universe
will collapse
if dark matter obscures
the visible stuff
we can pick up and play ball with –
or balance on the tip of the tongue
like a little bird –
is not what I am in the business of doing.

You may then ask
why it is I stand before you
conducting all manner of symphonies
from household objects,
in all possible permutations
of their seemingly rigid
and commonplace forms.
Think of me as just a juggler,
not princess of all gravity at all

but a juggler –
showing you the possibilities
of how space can be filled.
Not knowing the precise calculations
of all trajectories –
simply playing.
Now it's up to you to watch the little bird
on the tip of your tongue;
and if it takes flight, to follow.

Map

Animals grow up from the ground
so we might write on their skin
the story of the world,
this history that we own;
these impossible monsters
and all of the stars in heaven.

At the centre of this,
our house floats like a raft
above the nesting rats
and the heart of the burning earth;
that angry giant
with pestle and mortar.

We are careful in our navigation
that none of this is disturbed.
We are careful that even
the soles of our shoes
with their caterpillar tracks
shall not succumb to corruption.

We chain all our books
with their animal skin pages
to heavy desks and immovable objects.
We pray that this learning
is not taken away
by dark feathered birds of the night.

Stone

The sound of the bird
hitting the window
shocked the heavy air
of an August morning
like a stone thrown
into a boiling pan.

All day she avoided
looking out of the window,
but carried the sound
like a knife wedged
between her second
and third ribs.

All day, sixteen crows
circled the chimney,
the house, her throat
as a tightly wound choker.
By early evening
she could take it no more.

She flung open the door
and saw with her own eyes
her body askew on the patio,
all bent out of shape,
her favourite dress
spilling around her.

And this is when
she grew wings.
It wasn't simple –
they were rent from her back
with all the agony
of a slow and natural birth.

She should fly now –
it would be the logical end to the tale.
But that would be too easy.
Instead we watch her
walk into surrounding fields,
birth-blood dripping into dry earth.

Advice from the Third Little Pig

Not wise to build your house from sticks or straw
and so you need to heed my good advice
unless you want the wolf outside your door.

It's true that bricks and blocks will cost you more,
but bacon must be saved at any price –
not wise to build your house from sticks or straw.

Concrete just must be used, you can't ignore
the peace of mind it gives – so safe and nice.
Or do you want the wolf outside your door?

Beware that snarling gnashing carnivore,
his blazing eyes, his teeth, his heart of ice.
Not wise to build your house from sticks or straw.

These limp attempts at housing – are you *sure*
they'll not come crashing down in a trice?
Can't you see the wolf outside your door?

Your life is built upon a fatal flaw –
you want to be his latest sacrifice?
Not wise to build your house from sticks or straw,
unless you want the wolf outside your door.

Raindancing

Thunder paced the valley all night
keeping the chickens awake.
Lightning splintered the sky
and my house took its last breath
as everything plunged into darkness.

My eyes adapted easily
and my hearing grew very alert
when not distracted by
the house's heartbeat
and the humming in its veins.

It seemed more natural now
to move around on all fours,
making the cats in the kitchen
look askance as I slunk past
their milk bowl, heading for the cat-flap.

Even in this new state of affairs
it was apparent to me
that I was too big to get through,
so I unlocked the door
with my still dextrous paws.

It was cats and dogs outside
and the air was alive
with so many smells
that I sneezed several times
before I got used to it.

The garden fence was easy –
I climbed it in one leap.
Behind me, the house awoke,
while I scanned the fields
and the frogs raindancing in the grass.

Stealing Berries from the Birds

You must ignore
phantom magpies
eyeing up the broccoli;
you have no business with them.

You must ignore
the rising sun
the orange sky
and any other prettiness.

Duelling pheasants
should not bother you;
it is essential
that every nerve is alert.

Beware
the setting moon,
the warning clack
of blackbirds.

Lie low,
keep your ear to the ground.
Avoid the morning dew.
Carry a silver dish.

The man in the field with a broom

lives in the tall thin house
on the edge of the train track
with its long thin garden and intricate rows
of cabbages and brassicas.

He spends his days
sweeping the wheat fields clean,
worrying the hedgerows
for branches and leaves out of place.

Instead of his heart
there's a rock that
thwacks at the walls of his chest
like a fist.

And if the phone ever rings
there'll be nobody there,
just the cackle of static
itching the drum of his ear.

In the Glass Room

Her words were tiger-moths.
They eddied about his head
and fled towards
the cold glass walls.

He spoke laughing birds;
they gobbled up some
tiger-moths,
while chortling to themselves.

She cried snowflakes –
a powdery blizzard
settling around the room
in deep soft drifts.

She hollowed out a space
and climbed inside.
He watched in flummoxed silence
but was nowhere to be seen.

The moths bruised their wings
battering against the glass.
Laughing birds rolled around,
gleefully gripping their sides.

The Disappearing

Slowly he watched her disappear:
The empty pile where there used to be ironing,
the absence of lipstick on her coffee cup,
the plants, dry from wanting.

Her conversation became vague:
she would sit motionless in front of unlit fires,
talking in circles about boats she once owned
and lions that ate from the palm of her hand.

At the start of her disappearing
she would spend all day in the kitchen,
whisking up exotic meals from recipes
she said she'd learned from foreign shores.

But as her disappearing became more pronounced
she avoided the kitchen entirely.
So he made sturdy broths to feed her up
when her bones began to show.

Although by now she had stopped talking,
she would stand at the tall window,
dreamily singing songs he'd never heard;
songs that sounded less and less like earthly music.

One morning, when he was on the edge of sleep,
a soft fluttering persuaded him awake.
And there she was – a translucent shape
hovering at the open window.

He tried hopelessly to catch her ankle
as she drifted outside into the dawn light,
where already birds in their thousands
were gathering in the sky.

Missing You Spell

Today I will conjure you from thin air
using a strand of your hair
I found on the pillow
and two drops from the vial of your blood
I keep in the fridge door.

These things I will add to boiling water
with a few sprigs of rosemary
and a teaspoon of virgin honey.
I will chant your name in 13 languages;
I will dance to the music of this.

Then I will drink it down
from the biggest glass I can find.
I will drink until I do not belong to me.
And as the sweetness burns
right down to my stomach

I will feel your kisses at my throat,
your fingers pressing at my skin,
your tongue caressing every cell
every dark pathway
and hallowed cave of my body.

Next door is used to this.
They no longer call round
to ask why the walls are shaking.
They no longer question the animal cries
escaping through cracked kitchen windows.

Of the True Solution of Pearls

I am mixing a tincture
to cure the swimmings of my head
and give strength and comfort
to my poor little heart.

My very marrow is all messed up,
my bones don't seem to know me;
I'm a girl in a tizz,
bursting to dispel this distemper.

It's like a possession, I guess.
Your lips, your eyes, inside my skull;
your heart, your pulse,
inside my ears like the sea.

I have begun to pop one by one,
a string of pearls into a glass body
with the spirit of wine and sulfur;
they dissolve with a fizz.

I must have a quietening, a stilling,
I add cinnamon to the mix –
if anyone could see me,
they'd say I was doolally.

Apples and Stars

Your face is melting into her face,
the room spins three-sixty;
there are birds and sirens everywhere.
The sofa is on the ceiling;
you wade through the stars,
skin glowing in the swirl of the milky way.
Whole bowlfuls of fruit are consumed.
You bake cakes of each other and eat them.

There are reasons for this.
Scientific facts and chemical reactions.
Do not be disturbed –
your life will carry on much as before.
Once there are no more apples.
Once there are no more stars.

Gone

Each touch, my skin giggles
under your fingertips. My teeth
want to feel each tender morsel; your toes,
your ears, your willing lips, the nape
of your neck. Each touch and we are gone
deeper into each other

      until suffocated in sweetness this attic
room with its slow heat, its pillow
of air that it is not air that rises smooth
into our lungs as we breathe the burn
of each other, as we taste the sweat
that tastes of nothing else but water
that rises from the earth, that holds us
in some timeless place all afternoon.

Is This Okay?

Soundlessly,
I transform myself into light.
You have not noticed, it seems;
your breathing is untouched
as I hover above you.

My fingers brush your skin,
inventing new colours
we shall later name.
As my draping hair
describes the curve of your neck

your sleeping lips smile
and I fall in love again;
I am helpless to this.
Now I want to flood you completely
forgetting gentle patterns

forgetting the hovering
and the soundlessness.
I want to sing your name
until my whole essence –
or being or soul or whatever

you'd like to call it,
the whole of me and the whole of you –
are seamlessly joined, forever.
Maybe I should wake you
and at least ask if that's okay.

Honeymoon

The coat you have put on
to shield you from the waterfall
has fallen down from your shoulders, your head.
Your face is wet and smiling.

Behind us are countless strangers
and gallon upon gallon of crashing water.
We are lost in its tongue. This is heaven.

Flat

It wasn't the first time she'd taken
the entire contents from her flat
backwards over the welcome mat
and sat them on the lawn. Unshaken

the neighbours simply twitched
their curtains to see what this time
was in her mind, if any rhyme
or reason could be duly unhitched

from the tangle of this particular
morning's activity. Minutes later,
much rumbling and black smoke later,
it seemed the show was to be vehicular.

The steam roller lurched into view
from the high street. The ground
shivered, an odd whirring sound
came from the machine and through

the smoke, she could be picked out
riding high in the driver's seat wearing
a plastic headscarf and goggles staring
at the runway of her belongings. Without

flinching, full steam ahead she went,
to the cry of tally-ho! The standard lamp
was the first victim of this vicious revamp,
then the sofa, a table, a bucket; bent

up and broken beyond all redemption.
A birdcage, sans parrot, a bowl without fishes,
a sideboard full of her mother's dishes;
every last object without exemption

it seemed, was suddenly splendidly rendered.
She climbed to the roof for better perspective
in order to see just how effective
her efforts had been, what had surrendered

itself up to the wrath of the roller. Just
her dressmaker's mannequin stood
apart, naked, proud, looking as if it could
take on the whole world and more, dust

settling on its shoulders. It was round
about then that she slumped to her knees;
her wherewithal, loose change and keys
escaped her person and fell to the ground.

The neighbours say they watched her disappear,
but it's hard to believe everything you hear.

The Size of Kittens

Today I have seen
snowflakes the size of kittens,
heard the yelps
of a hundred million wood ants
from a village on the other side of the world
I don't even know the name of.

Heard the yelps
of a hundred million wood ants
as a kettle of hot water
the size of twenty kittens
was poured
slowly onto them.

Heard the yelps
and translated them into kitten language
then into the Queen's English
only to realise that it's OK –
that the wood ants are far too hardy
to let boiling water get them down.

And now the streets
are littered with kitten snow,
joining their paws
to cover everything,
making everything
into everything else.

Across the other side of the world
the ants carry on about their business.

Waiting for the Kettle to Boil

That a teaspoon could be made so unteaspoonlike;
mangled into a grimace, rendered cock-eyed
for the whole wide world to see, and cry
This is not a teaspoon! certainly makes you think.

Not least about perceptions and stuff.
After all, the same sliver of silver, if you pardon
the pun, is still there in your hands
and there's no reason why it could not still be

a teaspoon, now, is there? And that makes
you think about tenses and language. *Could be*
suggests oceans of possibilities,
and before you know it, you are stirring your tea

with a silver bullet and the whole shebang
of language and objects are ricocheting
from the painted walls inside your head,
and all you wanted was a cup of tea.

Clue

You hadn't meant to be alone –
you didn't plan for it.
It's just the train stopped moving
and everyone got off.
Except you.

There is plenty to look at;
cows, fields, babbling brooks,
England's garden
blossoming wonderfully
this late spring.

There's even a crossword
spread out on the table,
and look, you have a pen
in your hand, all ready
to fill in the blanks.

The train moves off, silently.
And the cows watch
your soundless scream
as you're carried away,
answers scrawled all over

your freshly ironed shirt;
*2 down: A fish swims backwards
into the slowly drifting snow
while up above, the scowling clouds
are swirling, endlessly.*

I Want To Be a Mad Woman

I want to be a mad woman
and have mad woman hair
that's all knotted and tied
up with daisy-chains.

I want to walk around barefoot
through fields and even
along the high street, not caring
about grass-stains and broken glass.

I want to be a mad woman
and live in the attic; keep bats
and laugh hysterically at their jokes
all through the night.

I want to start fires;
to watch armchairs and curtains
dissolve into carpets,
and lampshades melt into air.

I want you to be one of my delusions;
a figment, a hoax, a red herring.
And all the things you say
just to be voices in my head.

I could take tablets then,
to erase you chemically from my head.
I could whirl around in the sky
and not fall over the clouds.

For His Amusement

She turns herself into a small cat,
winds her body round his legs,
bakes cakes that fill the air with the taste of home.
Her whiskers try to be alert to atmospheric changes
that may avoid her feeling a boot in the ribs.

Sometimes, she is a pariah dog
snuffling at the corners of her room.
He doesn't favour this, tries to lure her back.
She returns as a drawer full of broken mousetraps
he wishes he could take back to the shop.

Dear John,

OK, well, when I said forever,
I was obviously being
very optimistic, wasn't I?
I mean, forever is a bloody
long time
if you think about it.

Even seas freeze over
eventually don't they?
And those giant turtles,
the ones who have, like,
one heartbeat an hour –
they cark it when their time comes.

So it's just kind of
a natural thing really;
rhythms and timescale and stuff.
The tide comes in and brings
bits and bobs onto the beach
then, sooner than you can blink,

it takes them all away again.
That's the way it goes, yeah?
So I've taken the Merc;
you know I hate public transport.
And I've taken the sun,
the stars and the moon.

They were presents, right?

Home Cooking

I'll take your eyes first
and boil them whole for the stock.
So you won't see what I do
with your family recipe,
how I boil for far too long
and consequently burn the pan.

How I don't slice carrots,
but your fingers instead.
I'll need a very sharp knife
but it can be done.
Just think of the wonderful crunch
those small bones would make.

And consider the possibility of ears;
how delicate on the plate.
I'll reserve those for desert,
cover them with
chocolate sauce,
arranging them, just so.

I would serve red wine,
an earthy un-oaked '99
with plenty of body
I've been saving
for such an occasion;
I think it would be to your taste.

Guest House

The fish are all eyes to this matinee,
this unfolding of the day
with its own particular fiction.

The teddy bears on the stairs,
the two sewing-machines shored up,
needles poised on this cushion of silence.

Outside, the sound of children playing,
in the carless sunny tree-lined streets,
where surely it is safe to play.

Inside, these mannequins
like chalk-lines drawn in air
are set to take your coats.

So take your shoes off,
the fish will guide you to your room.
See the graceful way they have

of shutting windows tight.

Welcome

What kind of a box is this
with three hundred pairs of legs
and no room to move
not even an inch?

And what kind of a journey
when three hundred pairs of eyes
have nothing to see
but the backs of their own heads?

What lies have been told
to get this box into the sea
with all its heartbeats
and lungs full of poison air?

Where will it wash up
but on a beach with wooden stakes,
some buried to their waists,
some buried to their necks?

Shelter

A grid of windows
rises up to be counted
above the frozen street.

Rooms like empty boxes
wait for a heartbeat
to shiver inside them.

The woman in the bus shelter
waits, and is waiting.

Salt

Not grain by grain
but a whole ocean;
dense and static.

I looked back just once
as sulfur fires
took our house.

Now salt is in me
and around me;
my name shall be salt.

Foolish woman
that I am,
see how I float!

See how your laws
of drowning
cannot contain me.

See how I am
the fixed
body of the earth

and how your angels,
are just young men
with painted wings.

Diet

It wasn't enough that the ark that I made
was easily sufficient for me to stow away
everything that I thought I knew. If I paid
attention to my instincts and felt the sway
of the ground below me. If I had just raised
my face and breathed in the swelling air –
I would have smelled the honey everywhere.
Then when it hit me, I wouldn't be so dazed.

Nor are umbrellas, sou'westers or galoshes
enough to deal with the oncoming tide
of you, my love. When your sweetness washes
beyond all my reason, I'm fair starry-eyed.
And I just want more, more, more, I tell you.
And low calorie sweeteners will simply not do.

Miscible

O won't you curve the meniscus of my dead sea
with your love which is like warm rainwater
which is like silk, which is like love
which is like breathing yet nothing else at all.

Talk to me in rainfall, think of me as a river bed
in the heat of summer; empty, baked, longing
for saturation, straining at the leash to be liquid again;
to dissolve, to become your element.

Come, my pretty – there is nothing to stop you now.
The small fishes of my hands are waiting to greet you.
They have been waiting for such a long time,
they think that maybe they've dreamt you.

Constellation

Ground

This square garden with its brick-square
walls is kept private from the field
of cows that floats above the river. There,
on the far bank is a pink house whose well-heeled
owners breed pampered dogs and horses
that live lives of Riley. But we all do round here,
in our big houses, our dinner parties, our four courses,
and champagne in the fridge. So much is clear
and unsaid. The herb garden does its thing,
the runner beans keep on running for want or
knowledge of anything else to do. We cling
to our clocks that never tick and close the door.

*

Somewhere outside the garden, something breathes
warm summer air. Something has willed
itself into being, is moving quickly through sheaves
of well kept wheat, through hen- and sheep-filled
meadows. If you listen past the usual night-time
music, past the river's gentle play as if your life
depended on it, if you put on your boots and climb
to the top of the hill you will hear night turn on a knife-
edge. How easily it's done. How simply the blade
is flicked. The breathing thing is swift on its two feet;
the simple wooden fences, the gates that you have made
are not enough, and it's far too late now, to retreat.

*

Inside this square garden with its brick-square
walls, the Minotaur is in his element. The neatly
planted rows of onions and carrots have taken a fair
battering. It is well past him to notice how sweetly
the air smells of crushed herbs, or to notice that he
has rose thorns in his feet. The dangerous mist
in front of his eyes masks every subtlety.

Just in case we haven't got the gist
of what is happening, the Minotaur directs his rage
at the conservatory. The glass sprinkles terrible rough
confetti over the lovage seedlings. If this were a page
in a book, it couldn't be turned quick enough.

String

She would always be on the look-out for string.
String of any length and weft; old bits of yarn
left out in the garden, new silky bits of darn
in rainbow colours, odd snags of sacking
from bags of potatoes – just kicking about by
the runner-beans or cut-offs from tethers
meant to keep stalks in an altogether
upright position. She didn't know why,
it's just something she has always done,
weaving them in some kind of narrative of string.
Today she'd find out why she would do such a thing.
Gosh, was she in for some fun!

*

The Minotaur was exhausted. He had by now
made a mockery of the whole garden.
She saw him from the broken window, fallen
apples all round him. He was trying somehow
to pick the rose thorns from his feet.
She couldn't think of what else to do, so
put the kettle on. And even though
he still looked quite fierce, decided to heat
up a few teacakes in the Aga. She saw no obstacle
and was certain that after a nice cup of tea
he would calm down, open his eyes, see
what he had done, and regret the whole spectacle.

*

But how to get him inside. He was clearly
a feral creature, more at home in the open air.
But she could simply not bear

the idea of her best china in the garden. Really,
that would be the last straw! But the string!
The string! That's what it was for! She collected
it all from the foot of her wardrobe. How unexpected,
she thought, pulling on her Wellingtons, heading
for the back door. The Minotaur raised
his heavy head as he heard the door close.
The summer air was heady and thick with rose-
scent and he sat among the wreckage, dazed.

*

He was docile as she began to wind the string around
his neck and shoulders, loosely so it wouldn't hurt
him. He looked very forlorn, sitting there in the dirt,
watching her as she circled him. Round and round
and round she went until she was quite dizzy.
She was seeing stars at this point. He saw them too –
they seemed to rest in her hair like a crown; the black-blue
of her hair, the night sky. They were so busy
with the circling and the stars, that had cajoled
them into this trance – they were not aware
of the shrill whistle of the kettle or anything, anywhere.
But she remembers leading him over the threshold.

Spell

Inside the walls had disappeared, the ceiling gone.
Inside the sky opened out above them,
and everything before this time that had been done
was now undone. Unravelling, even the hem
of her dress, forgot itself. The pearls of her necklace
formed a constellation that whirled round their heads.
They were the very centre of all this space.
And gravity, if it existed at all, was unread.

Somewhere on the edge of space, the song of rain
began to play. It grew nearer, the gentlest gentlest sound;
it was the hush of blood in their veins,
it was the sky come down to meet the ground.

*

Give me this flood, this timelessness.
Give me this slow saturation, this drowning.
Give me these cadences this foreign tongue.
Let the earth rip apart;
Let it swallow us whole, let it enter us.
Let the whole weight of the sky lift us up.
Let birds be mystified by our fluency.
Let the mirror of my skin show you your human face.
Give me the breath from your lungs;
Give me the beat of your heart;
Give me your name, scratch it into my skin.

The house, the garden, far out of sight
they found themselves beside a sky blue sea.
The sand – an unreal and sparkling white –
counted their footsteps. Time spun free,
they looked and saw there was nothing
between them; the same animal, same person.
The tide waited as it had waited, breathing
as it had breathed. Its quiet passion
drawing them closer. So close they were,
their feet sank deep into the wet sand.
And they carried on and on into the blur,
between sea and sky, sea and land.

*

This hush, this pulse, this moon-ruled place,
these stars, this dance, these circling stars.